KITES
BIRDS OF PREY
BY NATHAN SOMMER

EPIC

BELLWETHER MEDIA • MINNEAPOLIS, MN

EPIC BOOKS are no ordinary books. They burst with intense action, high-speed heroics, and shadows of the unknown. Are you ready for an Epic adventure?

This edition first published in 2019 by Bellwether Media, Inc.

No part of this publication may be reproduced in whole or in part without written permission of the publisher. For information regarding permission, write to Bellwether Media, Inc., Attention: Permissions Department, 6012 Blue Circle Dr. Minnetonka, MN 55343.

Library of Congress Cataloging-in-Publication Data

Names: Sommer, Nathan, author.
Title: Kites / by Nathan Sommer.
Description: Minneapolis, MN : Bellwether Media, Inc., 2019. | Series: Epic.
   Birds of Prey | Audience: Age 7-12. | Audience: Grade 2 to 7. | Includes
   bibliographical references and index.
Identifiers: LCCN 2018003577 (print) | LCCN 2018006815 (ebook) | ISBN
   9781626178779 (hardcover : alk. paper) | ISBN 9781681036274 (ebook)
Subjects: LCSH: Red kite–Juvenile literature. | Birds of prey–Juvenile
   literature.
Classification: LCC QL696.F32 (ebook) | LCC QL696.F32 S665 2019 (print) | DDC
   598.9–dc23
LC record available at https://lccn.loc.gov/2018003577

TABLE OF CONTENTS

ACROBATIC HUNTER

The snail kite circles low over the pond. It twists and turns, scanning the area for food.

This graceful bird puts on a show in flight. But it is actually a hungry **predator** about to make a kill!

5

The kite goes from flying a straight path to a sharp turn in an instant. Then, it swoops down!

6

The predator plucks a snail from the water without landing. Kites prefer their **prey** on the go!

WHAT ARE KITES?

SWALLOW-TAILED KITE

Kites are medium-sized birds of prey with long, pointed wings. Many have forked tails.

These birds are known for being **agile** in flight. They often **glide** through the sky without flapping their wings.

RED KITE

BLACK KITE

There are more than 20 types of kites in the world. They **adapt** to most warm **habitats**.

Kites like to hunt in low, open areas where they can easily find food. They nest on tree branches, cliffs, or buildings.

TYPES OF KITES

MISSISSIPPI KITE

RED KITE

WHITE-TAILED KITE

SWALLOW-TAILED KITE

CLEVER CARNIVORES

BLACK-SHOULDERED KITE

These **carnivores** hunt small prey. Most kites eat insects like grasshoppers and beetles. Larger kites snack on mice and voles.

Some kites hunt prey that are difficult to eat. Snail kites have special hooked beaks to break snail shells!

SNAIL KITE

A Stinging Snack

Some kites enjoy eating wasps. They will fly off with whole wasp nests!

Fire Starters

Scientists believe some kites spread wildfires. The birds purposely drop burning sticks into grass where they feed. Then, they catch escaping prey!

Kites lack the strength of other birds of prey. They make up for it by being smart, **alert** hunters.

The birds fly low to track their prey. They use **talons** to snatch it up without landing.

15

Fly a Kite

"Kiting" lets kites stay in one place in midair. The birds turn into the wind and flutter their wings. Toy kites do this too!

WHISTLING KITE

Long tails allow kites to be **acrobatic** hunters. They use them to change direction in a split second.

Sometimes, the birds dive backward to catch food behind them. Prey has a tough time getting away.

CARRION

Other kites are **scavengers**. Many eat trash and **carrion**. In cities, the birds are known to steal food from people's hands!

Clever kites rarely miss a meal.
These graceful hunters are masters
of the sky!

BRAHMINY KITE

WHITE-TAILED KITE PROFILE

RED LIST STATUS: LEAST CONCERN

LEAST CONCERN	NEAR THREATENED	VULNERABLE	ENDANGERED	CRITICALLY ENDANGERED	EXTINCT IN THE WILD	EXTINCT

AVERAGE LIFE SPAN: UP TO 6 YEARS
GREATEST HUNTING TOOL: LONG, POINTED WINGS
WINGSPAN: UP TO 3.5 FEET (1 METER)

WHITE-TAILED KITE RANGE MAP

WHITE-TAILED KITE RANGE =

PREY

VOLES	LIZARDS	MICE	GRASSHOPPERS

GLOSSARY

acrobatic—like an acrobat; acrobats perform tricks for an audience while high up in the air.

adapt—to change over time to more easily survive

agile—able to move quickly and easily

alert—aware of what is happening nearby

carnivores—animals that only eat meat

carrion—the rotting meat of a dead animal

glide—to fly smoothly, without flapping the wings very much

habitats—the homes or areas where animals prefer to live

predator—an animal that hunts other animals for food

prey—animals that are hunted by other animals for food

scavengers—animals that mostly eat food that is already dead

talons—the strong, sharp claws of kites and other birds of prey

TO LEARN MORE

At the Library

Hoena, Blake. *Everything Birds of Prey*. Washington, D.C.: National Geographic, 2015.

Riggs, Kate. *Vultures*. Mankato, Minn.: Creative Education, 2015.

Sommer, Nathan. *Hawks*. Minneapolis, Minn.: Bellwether Media, 2019.

On the Web

Learning more about kites is as easy as 1, 2, 3.

1. Go to www.factsurfer.com.

2. Enter "kites" into the search box.

3. Click the "Surf" button and you will see a list of related web sites.

With factsurfer.com, finding more information is just a click away.

INDEX

The images in this book are reproduced through the courtesy of: Rafal Szozda, front cover; Paolo-manz, p. 2; mark smith nsb, pp. 4, 5, 6, 7; LagunaticPhoto, pp. 8, 11 (bottom right); fernando sanchez, pp. 9, 11 (top left); RUPA GHOSH/ Alamy, p. 10; Erni, p. 11 (top right); Phoo Chan, p. 11 (bottom left); David Whelan/ Alamy, p. 12; Andrew M. Allport, p. 13; EcoPrint, p. 14; Abhishek S Padmanabhan, p. 15; Heather Ruth Rose, p. 16; Andrew Astbury, p. 17; Bildagentur Zoonar GmbH, p. 18; Wang LiQiang, p. 19; win247, p. 20; Cindy Creighton, p. 21 (left); Joseph M. Arseneau, p. 21 (left middle); Rudmer Zwerver, p. 21 (right middle); Eve Wehrli, p. 21 (right).